SEEING SCIENCE THROUGH ART

Sky Tree

THOMAS LOCKER

with

CANDACE CHRISTIANSEN

HarperCollins*Publishers*

To Terence

The illustrations for this book were painted with
oils on canvas.

Sky Tree
Seeing Science Through Art
Copyright © 1995 by Thomas Locker Inc.
Printed in the U.S.A. All rights reserved.

Library of Congress Cataloging-in-Publication Data
Locker, Thomas.
   Sky tree: seeing science through art / by Thomas Locker ; with
questions and answers by Candace Christiansen
      p.   cm.
   ISBN 0-06-024883-1. — ISBN 0-06-024884-X (lib. bdg.)
   1. Trees—Juvenile literature.   2. Seasons—Juvenile literature.
[1. Trees.   2. Seasons.]   I. Christiansen, Candace.   II. Title.
QK475.8.L64   1995   94-38342
582.16—dc20   CIP
                                                                AC

Book design by Tom Starace
1 2 3 4 5 6 7 8 9 10
❖
First Edition

AUTHOR'S NOTE

I have spent most of my life learning to paint trees against the ever changing sky. After all these years I still cannot look at a tree without being filled with a sense of wonder.

Since I began collaborating with Candace Christiansen, who is a science teacher, I have become increasingly aware of the scientific approach to the natural world. I was amazed to discover that the more scientific facts I learned, the deeper my sense of wonder became. This realization led to the creation of *Sky Tree*.

Sky Tree invites adults and children to experience the life of a tree and its relationship to the sky in several different ways. Through storytelling, art appreciation, and scientific exploration, *Sky Tree* attempts to reach both the heart and the mind.

—T. L.

*O*nce a tree

stood alone on a hill by

the river. Through the

long days, its leaves

fluttered in the soft

summer breeze.

When you look at this painting of the tree on a hill, can you remember how you felt on a perfect summer day?

But then the days grew shorter and the nights longer. The winds became cold, and the tree began to change.

This is the same tree in the same place. What makes this painting different?

Autumn came.
The leaves of the tree
turned gold, orange, and
red. Squirrels hurried to
store nuts and
acorns.

What does this painting show us about autumn colors?

*T*he sun rose later
each day. One morning,
light glistened on a thin
silver frost. By the end of
the day, many leaves
began to fall, first one
and then another.

Why does this painting make you feel sad? Is the tree dying?

On a grey day, an old snapping turtle buried herself in the river mud, where she would sleep until spring. The tree's bare branches reached toward the sky. The clouds opened, and for a moment, the sky filled the branches.

Why is this painting so strange and startling?

On a misty morning, a flock of birds landed where the tree's leaves had been. The birds chirped, squabbled, and sang, but suddenly their wings beat the air, and they flew away.

How does this painting capture the feeling of a misty day?

Clouds gathered
and filled the tree's
empty branches
and then drifted
away.

*How does this painting show how water in the air
changes the way we see things?*

*I*ce formed on the
river's edge. With its
roots deep in the earth,
the tree stood ready
for winter.

Does this painting make you feel as if something is about to happen?

Snows fell.
Snug in their nest, a
family of squirrels
huddled close through
the cold winter days.

How does this painting capture the stillness of a snowy day?

At night, millions of stars twinkled among the branches of the tree. Beneath the river ice, the old snapping turtle slept. The world was waiting for spring.

Does this painting make you feel small?

Late one afternoon,
a golden light streamed
through the clouds and
warmed the tree.
The ice on the river
began to melt, and the
snow disappeared into
the ground.

How does this painting show that winter is ending?

The smell of wet earth filled the air. Squirrels raced through the fresh grass and up the tree. Sap rose to the tree's tight buds.

Does this painting make you feel hopeful?

The old snapper crawled

out of the mud to lay her eggs

on the warm hillside.

The tree's leaves uncurled in

the spring sunlight, and the

birds returned to build nests for

their young.

Now the tree is full and round again. What does this painting make you feel about summer?

The tree stood on the hill by the river. Once again, its leaves fluttered in the soft summer breeze.

Why do you think this book is called Sky Tree?

CONNECTING ART AND SCIENCE IN *SKY TREE*

THE SUMMER TREE

When you look at this painting of the tree on a hill, can you remember how you felt on a perfect summer day?

Summer is a gentle time of year filled with greens and sparkling sunlight. How does the painter remind you of that feeling? Look at the lines around the clouds. There are none. The summer blue sky meets the white of the clouds, and the edges are blended softly. The painter chose greens that are in harmony with the blues. Throughout the painting there are small sparkling highlights that suggest sunlight. It is this light that the tree uses in combination with air, earth, and water to make all of the food it needs to live and grow.

THE CHANGE TREE

This is the same tree in the same place. What makes this painting different?

The painting of the Summer Tree is filled with light and softly blended colors. Using the same subject, the artist has created a different mood. This painting is abrupt and dark. Browns and blacks move quickly from dark to light. Tiny white brush strokes give the sense of the leaves upturned by the wind. This painting shows us that the tree's environment is changing as the seasons change. When the seasons change, all living things change in response.

THE AUTUMN TREE

What does this painting show us about autumn colors?

This painting is about color—clashing color. Orange is the opposite of blue in the color spectrum. The blue makes the orange seem even more orange. The painter has used the brightest pigments in his paint box to create the excitement and color of the fall. These bright colors are found in nature: the tree's leaves have always contained the orange and yellow pigments that now shine out. They were hidden beneath the green pigment, called chlorophyll, which made food for the tree during the long summer days.

THE RED TREE

Why does this painting make you feel sad? Is the tree dying?

The artist has painted the tree on the hill in a fading end-of-day light. The sky is painted in muted shades of red. The leaves have lost their brilliance, and so many have fallen that the tree looks like a skeleton. With the muted colors and the faded quality of light, the painter helps us to experience the somber feeling of autumn. The tree appears to be dying, but in truth, the tree sheds its leaves to help it retain water and survive the frozen winter days ahead.

THE SKY TREE

Why is this painting so strange and startling?

This painting does not make you feel sad like the Red Tree, or warm like the Summer Tree. The painter has placed a blue sky shape where the leaves were, and you probably wonder why. By choosing a puzzling image, and by using realistic color and line, the painter has crafted a painting that makes you wonder. The painting also makes you think about the relationship between the sky and the tree. Now that the tree is bare, you can see how the branches grow toward the light.

THE MIST TREE

How does this painting capture the feeling of a misty day?

All paints are made up of some finely ground stuff mixed with some more liquid substance, such as oil, water, or even the yolk of an egg. The paintings in this book were done with oil paint. Oil paint dries slowly. An artist can use his finger to blend it, and in this case, the artist took some light-grey paint and went over the painting with a soft brush to make the mist. This makes everything soft. In nature, mist often makes things hazy and hard to see.

THE CLOUD TREE

How does this painting show how water in the air changes the way we see things?

The mists in this painting are rising. The moisture in the air has collected on dust and salt particles to form clouds. You can see the mountains again, but they look far, far away. Why has the artist painted the mountains a bluish color? If you were to go to the mountains, you would find that they are covered by brown, not blue, trees. When you see something in the distance, you have to look through a lot of tiny particles of water that often make things look blue. This is one of the ways the artist made the mountains look far away.

THE VIOLET TREE

Does this painting make you feel as if something is about to happen?

The painter is using the same trick again. He has painted the sky so that it replaces the tree's leaves, but this time the sky is violet. The violet clashes in an unsettling way with the yellow at the horizon. It is getting dark. Perhaps the tense mood of the painting makes you feel worried about the tree. Winter is coming, but the tree is ready for it. The tree will survive because of its roots, which anchor it against strong winds and provide stores of food for the time of year when the tree cannot make its own food.

THE SNOW TREE

How does this painting capture the stillness of a snowy day?

A snowy day is quiet and muffled. The artist captures the silence of a winter's afternoon with a thousand shades of blue and silver. Unlike the Violet Tree, there are no clashing colors or sharp lines. Everything seems close-up and flat. The light is even and dim. Only the strong trunk of the tree stands out. It is the strength of the tree's trunk that makes it possible for it to bear the weight of the heavy snow.

THE STAR TREE

Does this painting make you feel small?

Some paintings are composed of big, simple forms. Others are made of tiny parts. In this painting, the artist made everything in the foreground out of focus. You look past the tree on the hill deep into space at an infinite number of stars, millions of miles away. Do you think, for a moment, about how small we are, and how vast the universe is?

THE GOLDEN SUN TREE

How does this painting show that winter is ending?

This painting shows the snow melting and the ice on the river breaking. The dark blue and grey colors of winter are past. From behind the dark cloud that once again fills the empty branches of the tree, rays of golden light link the sun to the earth. The light brightens the earth and lightens the mood of the painting. It causes the ice to melt and signals the tree to begin new growth again.

THE BUD TREE

Does this painting make you feel hopeful?

This painting almost makes you squint. The sun is just a small circle of white light, and the feeling of warmth is created by the soft yellows spreading gently into a blue spring sky. The artist has used the fresh greens and pinks of early spring days. You can almost feel the new warmth of the sun on your face. Both the text and the painting are filled with reminders of the first sensations of spring.

THE SUMMER TREE

Now the tree is full and round again. What does this painting make you feel about summer?

The artist has chosen this day in June to paint a hillside filled with golden dandelions. With amazing punctuality, snapping turtles begin to lay their eggs on the longest day of the year, which always comes in June. Birds are returning to build their nests against a gold and violet sky. The colors are rich and vibrant. The strong light of the summer sun is coming from the side of the painting, and it makes the tree appear full. The whole image, filled with life, has a sense of growth and new beginnings.

THE SUNSET TREE

Why do think this book is called Sky Tree?

The sky and the tree have a special relationship. During this year in the tree's life, it received light, air, and water from the sky. The tree, in turn, gave off water and oxygen to renew the sky. Because the life of the tree and the sky are so related, this book is called *Sky Tree*.

THOMAS LOCKER

was born in New York City in 1937. He started his art training at the age of six. In 1944 he won first prize in the children's division of the Washington, D.C., *Times Herald* art fair with a painting of a giant tree that still stands in the National Zoo. Thomas Locker received his B.A. in Art History from the University of Chicago and M.A. from American University. He studied and traveled in Europe, then taught art at several colleges in the Midwest and exhibited paintings at galleries, holding about forty-five one-man exhibitions in London, New York, Chicago, Los Angeles, and other art centers. In 1984 Mr. Locker created his first picture book, WHERE THE RIVER BEGAN. Since then he has completed twenty books, many of which have received awards like *The New York Times* Best Illustrated of the Year, American Library Association Best Books for Children, and the Christopher Award.

CANDACE CHRISTIANSEN

is a teacher of chemistry and mathematics at a school in Columbia County, New York. She is the author of three children's books: CALICO AND TIN HORNS, THE ICE HORSE, and THE MITTEN TREE. Ms. Christiansen has been a weaver, a shepherd, and has raised four children.

Thomas Locker and Candace Christiansen live in a little village on the edge of the Hudson River in a melded family that includes nine children (many are already grown up).